LIFE IN THE MIDDLE AGES™

THE LIVES OF WOMEN

MARGAUX BAUM AND
ANDREA HOPKINS, PH.D.

rosen publishing's rosen central®
NEW YORK

Published in 2017 by The Rosen Publishing Group
29 East 21st Street, New York, NY 10010

First Edition

Library of Congress Cataloging-in-Publication Data

Names: Baum, Margaux, author. | Hopkins, Andrea, author.
Title: The lives of women / Margaux Baum and Andrea Hopkins, Ph.D.
Description: First edition. | New York : Rosen Publishing, 2016. | Series: Life in the Middle Ages | Includes bibliographical references and index. | Audience: Grades 5-8.
Identifiers: LCCN 2016030409 | ISBN 9781499464665 (library bound)
Subjects: LCSH: Women—History—Middle Ages, 500-1500--Juvenile literature. | Middle Ages—Juvenile literature. | Civilization, Medieval—Juvenile literature.
Classification: LCC HQ1143 .B38 2016 | DDC 305.409/02—dc23
LC record available at https://lccn.loc.gov/2016030409

Manufactured in China

CONTENTS

INTRODUCTION

The status of women in modern societies, from the developing world to the industrialized, Western nations, remains ever-changing. However, many people agree that women's treatment as citizens and people has mostly improved in the last past century. Compare the way women are treated now to their treatment in 1920, the first year that women were guaranteed the right to vote in the United States after the enactment of the nineteenth amendment to the US Constitution. Think back further and consider the conditions under which women existed in the nineteenth century, or the fifteenth century.

Women have come a long way, especially compared to the lives most of them lived during the middle ages. European women who lived during the Middle Ages—from about 500 CE to 1500 CE—lived very differently from modern women. The cultures and societies of that era varied greatly, from Ireland in the west, to the Byzantine Empire of the east, from Iceland to Spain, and from Romania to the Baltic kingdoms. For the most part, however, men had greater rights, privileges, status, and power than women.

Medieval women in many areas of Europe generally had far greater restrictions on their roles and rights than nowadays. However, each region and nation differed. Some of the ethnic and national groups discussed in this book allowed women surprising independence. Others were more restrictive and even oppressive for its female members. Still, even those who did not enjoy the

The page depicted here is from the *Tacuinum Sanitatis*, a medieval handbook on good health and medical treatments. A peasant and her daughter gather maize, an ingredient in some treatments.

same rights and privileges as men were essential, and sometimes quite influential, members of their communities. This was true for both peasants who worked the land and landed members of the nobility (those who owned land and held political power).

What was it like for women in Medieval Europe? How they lived their lives, worked, earned a living, or helped their families get by can tell us much about not only women, but also about the society and culture of the time. We can also explore whether they had autonomy—that is, the power they had to make decisions about their own lives. The laws they lived under varied among different parts of Europe, and changed over time.

Medieval European women did housekeeping and were in charge of rearing children, but many of them did so much more. From being trusted advisers to their noble and royal spouses, to ruling in their own right, from acting as servants to actually being tradespeople, scholars, healers, and so much more. The experiences of women of this era is known to us through ancient writing and other works of art, and provides a fascinating glimpse of just how complex and nuanced the lives of women in the Middle Ages were.

CHAPTER ONE

WOMEN IN THE FAMILY

Women have been vital and active members of all societies from the dawn of history, even as they have, unfortunately, often been deemed second-class citizens. That women were seen as lesser than men was a feature of many civilizations of antiquity and was taken for granted in the first millennium CE. European culture proved no exception to these traditional beliefs. The roots of these beliefs go back not only to the ancient traditions of European peoples before Christianity, but were especially strengthened by the power of the Catholic Church. Christian ideals of womanhood had a major effect on what people found acceptable when it came to women's roles and rights. But women often rose above the limitations and the stereotypes that their cultures ascribed to them.

In medieval Europe, there was a powerful cultural tradition that saw men as better than women in every way. Men were thought to be not only physically stronger but also more emotionally stable, more intelligent, and morally less feeble. These ideas were taught by the church because they were at the root of the Old Testament. God tells Eve in the book of Genesis, "Your desire shall be for your husband, and he shall rule over you." Laws and customs defined what women could and could not do.

Although most people accepted these ideas about women, their work was essential and respected. Peasant women worked in the fields beside the men and were proud of their skills at the traditionally feminine crafts of spinning, weaving, dyeing, and sewing. Most people lived in small communities in the country and had to make all their own clothes and food. It was an accepted partnership in which men did most of the heavy outdoor work and women managed the house and yard. Women in towns could run their own businesses if they wanted, as well as help husbands and fathers with their specialized crafts. Women in the gentry and nobility managed estates and acted on behalf of their husbands in every possible way. Women who chose a religious life were also seen as making an essential contribution to society through their prayers and charitable acts.

Women could not be doctors, priests, judges, university professors, or lawyers. But they could be writers and artists, as well as craftswomen and tradeswomen. Many women were also believed to have prophetic visions. Their advice was eagerly sought and their views were respected. Sometimes, we think of the Middle Ages as being very distant and primitive. We forget that many of the institutions familiar to us in modern life—such as universities, parliaments, banks, and the social ideas of marriage and romantic love—were developed during the Middle Ages. The restriction of women to the tasks of housekeeping and child-rearing did not take effect until well into the modern era.

A QUESTION OF CLASS

Most women in medieval Europe expected to get married and have children. As far as we can tell from the records that survive, this is what the majority of women did. A medieval wife was her husband's partner in whatever work he did. If she was a peasant, she would sometimes help him in the fields, but she would spend most of her time working in the house and yard, looking after the chickens and pigs, spinning wool, making clothes, preparing food and drink, and looking after young children. If she was the wife of a craftsman or merchant, living in a town, she would supervise his workers and serve in the shop, as well as run the household. If she was married to a wealthy man or a nobleman, she would manage his estate in his absence and supervise and pay his workers. She would represent her lord in the courts by signing legal documents, in addition to the traditional duties of running the household and providing hospitality to visitors.

The great majority of people in medieval Europe were peasants who lived and worked in small communities in the countryside. They were farm workers who raised crops and animals and provided the basic foodstuffs for everyone in their society. Most of these people, while not technically slaves, were "unfree" in the sense that they could not choose where to live or what to do. They had

This tapestry shows a couple being married by a cleric, with their witnesses looking on. The bonds of marriage were enforced both socially and by the Roman Catholic faith of many western Europeans.

to stay in their village and work for their lord. Women had a little more freedom than men because they could move to a new community by marrying a man from another place. And peasant women had more freedom than noblewomen or middle-class women to marry someone they liked. A peasant woman's life consisted of hard work from the moment she awoke, at sunrise or even earlier, to the moment she collapsed into bed in the early evening. In rural communities there were no shops, and every household had to make and maintain everything it needed—heat, light, food, drink, clothes, and tools.

KEEPING HOUSE

A peasant woman's first chores of the day were to light a fire and draw water from the nearest well. Then she would milk whatever animals the family kept, such as cows, goats, or sheep. After that, she would set a pot of water on the fire and begin to make pease porridge in it. There were no potatoes in medieval Europe. The staple foods of most people were bread and a kind of vegetable stew made with whatever the wife grew in the

This image from the *Luttrell Pasalter* text shows women milking sheep in a pen, with others carrying the milk away.

yard—onions, leeks, peas, beans, herbs, and legumes. The wife would also make little cakes or scones. All the cooking was done in or over a fire with the help of a big cooking pot, called a cauldron, or a roasting spit. Every village would have at least one baking oven, and all the wives would bring their bread there at some point during the day to bake in it.

Once she had fed her husband and seen him off to work in the fields, the wife could tend to her children, clean her house and yard, wash and mend clothes, spin thread or weave cloth, and prepare food. She might churn butter, make cheese, salt meat or fish, and brew ale. Water was generally not safe to drink, and most people, including children, drank ale every day. Most peasant households brewed their own ale instead of buying it, but it was common to make more than was needed and supply some to other households. The neighbors would take turns brewing ale, and in this way, it was always available (it did not stay fresh for more than three days). In addition to all this work in and around the home, peasant women sometimes worked in the fields along with their husbands. At harvest time, every able-bodied person was needed to help bring in the crops. At other times, women helped by weeding, picking stones, sowing, and gleaning (gathering up bits of wheat left behind by the reapers at harvest), and sometimes by guiding the oxen as their husbands plowed.

Women who lived in towns and whose husbands were craftsmen with a specialized trade were usually better off than peasant women. They did not need

Another miniature excerpt from the *Tacuinum Sanitatis* shows women preparing tripe, one of the many food-related tasks that women of a certain class were usually proficient in.

to work in the fields, and they could afford to keep a servant or two to do the cleaning, child care, and basic food preparation. They also had more money to spend on items like clothes and crockery, rather than having to make everything. Town houses usually had a narrow front facing the street, but they extended a long way behind it. The ground floor of this long, narrow plot was usually a shop at the front, with a workshop in back, and behind the shop a yard that might contain a well and probably also the cesspit for all the household's domestic waste. (This is why

THE BOOK ON MEDIEVAL HOUSEKEEPING

There were several manuals written in the late Middle Ages for teaching young women how to be good housewives. These books were intended for middle-class women who could read and had received at least some education. These handbooks of practical advice give us a valuable picture of the ideas medieval people had about marriage and women. Most of the writers were men. One famous writer, however, was a woman named Christine de Pizan. She wrote a book called *The Treasure of the City of Ladies* in 1405. The goal of the housewife in Christine's book is to perform all her necessary tasks well, so that her husband will love and honor her and she will have the respect of everyone she deals with.

She wants to have the reputation of being a wise, sensible, reliable, intelligent, and virtuous woman. According to Christine, there is plenty of scope within married life for satisfaction. Here are some of the things she recommends for the middle-class wife:

The wise housewife ought to be very familiar with everything to do with preparing food, so that she can organize it the best way and give orders to her servants. In this way she will always be able to keep her husband contented. If he sometimes invites important people to the house, she herself ought, if necessary, to go to the kitchen and supervise the serving of food. She should make sure that her house is kept clean and everything is orderly and in its proper place. She should see that her children are well taught and disciplined, even if they are small, and that they are not heard whining or making a lot of noise. They should be kept tidy and established in their own routine. She must make sure that her husband's clothes and belongings are kept clean, for the good grooming of the husband is the honor of the wife. She must make sure that he is well served and has uninterrupted peace and quiet. Before he comes home for dinner everything should be ready and in good order, with tables and sideboards according to their means.

This and other manuals of instruction give a picture of the ideal housewife's life—a life of virtue, activity, and order. Her husband was the head of the household, and she deferred to him. But if she was good at her job, she enjoyed his confidence and respect.

the water was not safe to drink!) The family's living quarters were over the shop. The wife was in charge of the servants, and the husband was in charge of the apprentices who worked for him. These people would usually sleep on the ground floor where they worked. Wives of craftsmen often worked beside their husbands, especially if the husbands were in trades involving food, drink, cloth, or leather.

RAISING CHILDREN

Every wife was expected to bear children. Children were important in every marriage, whether rich or poor. If the family was wealthy and had property, there needed to be sons to inherit everything. If they were poor peasants, children were necessary to share the work of the parents and to increase the family's productivity. If a woman was unable to have children, she might find herself being divorced and put in a convent so that the husband could marry and have children with someone else. Even healthy women would often have problems getting pregnant. Often there were famines, or food shortages, caused by war, and many women, especially poorer ones, did not get enough to eat. A women may not be able to become pregnant if she is malnourished.

It was well known that having children was dangerous for women. Records of causes of death from the city of Florence show that in the year 1424, out of all the married women between the ages of twenty-five and thirty who died there, 20 percent had died in childbirth. Medieval medicine was based on an elaborate theory about how the body worked, why it went wrong, and how it could be cured. It was highly sophisticated, but it was wrong. Although all doctors were men, the care of pregnant women was a specialized area reserved for women known as midwives. These women were excluded from the education, training, and high social status given to male doctors, but they worked from a body of knowledge about childbirth based on centuries of experience and passed on from woman to woman. But no matter how knowledgeable or experienced a midwife was, there were still no anesthetics, no blood transfusions, no antibiotics, and—most dangerous of all—no concept of hygiene. Most mothers who died in childbirth either bled to death or suffered serious infections in the days following the birth.

It was universally accepted that the care of babies and small children was women's work. However, it was not high status work, and any woman who could afford it would hire other women to look after her babies and small children for her. Some women added to their family's income by breast-feeding other women's babies. These women were called wet nurses. Most mothers in northern Europe breast-fed their own babies and hired a wet nurse only if they were unable to do so. In southern Europe, it was the custom for better-off mothers to hire wet nurses to feed their babies. The usual arrangement was that the baby would be sent to live with the wet nurse's family

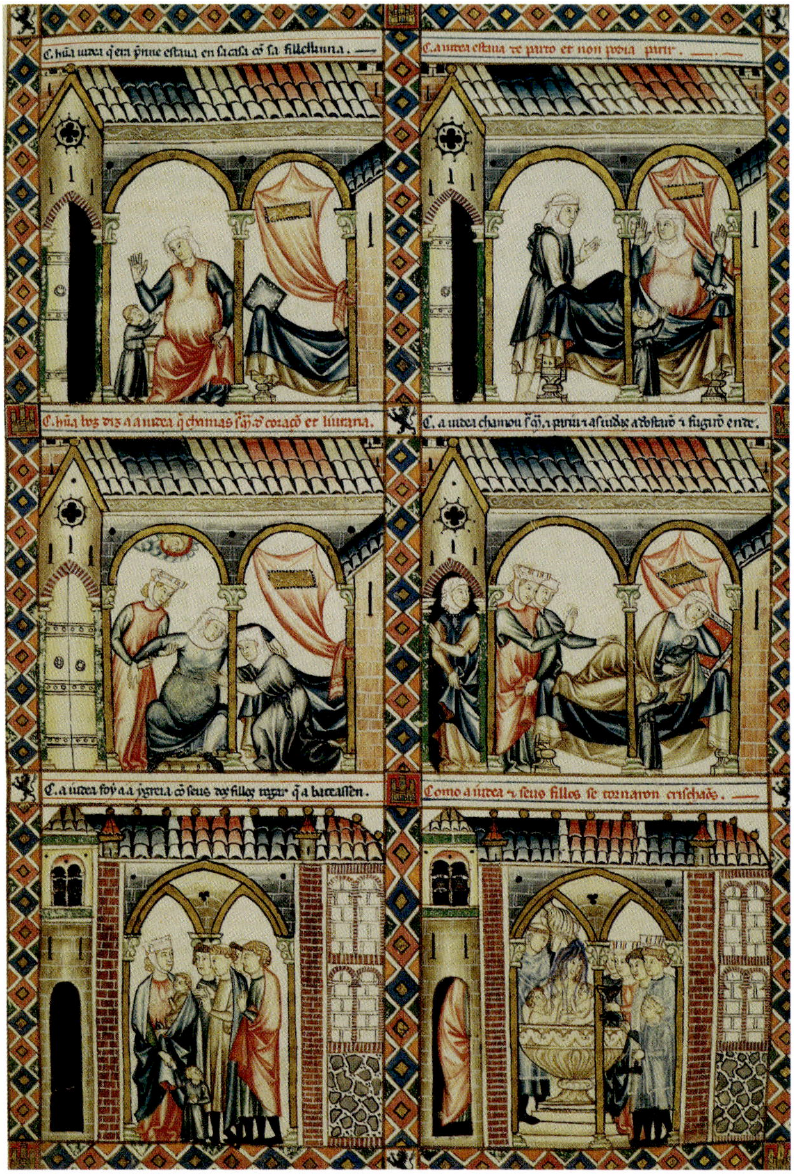

This manuscript illustration from the *Cantigas de Santa Maria*, created in Spain in the thirteenth century, depicts the stages of a woman giving birth and then the baptism of her child.

for the first year or two of its life. This was a popular choice for women who lived in towns. Towns could be very unhealthy and unsanitary places with a high risk of disease. A baby would be much better off staying in the home of a strong and healthy young peasant woman who lived in the countryside.

Children were the responsibility of their mothers until the age of seven. After that, their fate depended on their family's wealth and rank. Peasant children would begin to work beside their parents: girls in the house and yard, boys in the fields. Middle-class children might stay at home to work. If boys, they might be apprenticed to another master craftsman to learn his trade. Aristocratic children might be sent to the homes of wealthy and powerful relatives or to monasteries or convents if they were destined for the church.

Many babies and small children died. A combination of poor sanitation and poor diet meant that they fell ill easily and did not have the strength to survive. Modern historians used to think that medieval parents probably did not feel as attached to their babies as parents do nowadays because they were so likely to die. But there is no evidence for this. What evidence we have shows that mothers and fathers in medieval Europe loved their babies very much and grieved for them when they died. Children also suffered many accidents in and around the home. People in towns lived in upstairs rooms that had to be lit by candles and were full of flammable materials like straw, cloth, and wood. Records show that many children were burned to death in their cots in house fires. Many more were killed or injured by horses or carts when they were playing in the streets.

Being a medieval wife and mother was not easy. Some people thought it meant nothing but grief, ill health, and trouble. In several religious books, there were arguments aimed at persuading women that the religious life was much better than getting married. A husband and children were nothing but hard work and sorrow, these arguments went, and getting pregnant would make you horribly ill and destroy your good looks. Giving birth would be painful. A baby meant you wouldn't sleep nights for several years, you'd need to clean up all the baby's filth, your figure would be ruined, and you'd always be worried about your child. It was much more peaceful and agreeable to be a nun. But was it?

CHAPTER TWO

WOMEN OF THE NOBILITY

For women who were peasants, serfs, or any other kinds of commoners, life was tougher. Their counterparts in the nobility—and its highest reaches, royalty—lived more comfortably in every possible way. They were well-fed and pampered from birth, and thus more likely to grow strong and healthy, and avoid illnesses of all kinds. Their wealth, property, and station in life, along with their superior education, gave them every advantage in life. Still, they were constrained in other ways. For example, noblewomen were promised to grooms in arranged marriages from as young as five years old.

Because there were so many wars and invasions in the few hundred years following the collapse of the Roman Empire, much of European society was very unsettled. Many events are poorly documented in the historical record. There were massive invasions of southern and western Europe by Germanic tribes who conquered and settled England, France, Spain, and Italy during the fifth and sixth centuries. They had hardly settled down to rule over their new lands when another massive invasion by Islamic peoples from the south overran Spain and parts of Italy and almost conquered southern France. Eastern Europe was also under constant attack from various nomadic tribal peoples during this time. By the eighth century, the Norse-speaking peoples of northern Europe attacked their southern neighbors, too, and Viking armies made Christian Europe's life a misery for the next three hundred years.

FEMALE ROYALTY

In Germanic and Norse societies, especially pre-Christian ones, women of high status had much greater independence and freedom of choice in their lives than at any time since the twentieth century. In Anglo-Saxon England, for example, women could own property—meaning land, manors, and estates—and it remained theirs even after they got married. A married woman could leave her property to anyone she liked. In the late Middle Ages, a married woman's property became the property of her husband when she married. All that she could bequeath to others were her chattels, or movable goods such as clothes, jewels, furniture, linen, plates, and tools. Women in pre-Christian societies were allowed to divorce their husbands if they wished to by stating their intention to do so publicly, in front of witnesses, and men could divorce their wives by the same procedure. Several Arab writers who traveled in northern Europe commented on the freedom that women in Norse societies had to go where they wished, to address men face-to-face as equals, to conduct business, and to choose their own partners. They found this shocking but fascinating.

In Germanic societies, it was the custom for queens to be crowned separately from kings and to sit on thrones alongside their husbands on state occasions. Often a foreign king who had conquered a country would marry the queen of the king he had just killed because being the consort of the ruling

French noblewomen are shown in this illustration, depicted in finery. The crowned woman is Isabeau of Bavaria, who would marry Charles VI to become queen of France.

queen strengthened his claim to the throne. Thus, when King Cnut the Great of Denmark conquered England in 1017, he immediately made a political marriage to Queen Emma, the widow of King Ethelred of England. By all accounts, Emma was a very forceful woman. She even commissioned a rather flattering biography of herself called *Encomium Emmae* (Praise of Emma). Queens rarely ruled alone during this period, but it often happened that the reigning king was killed fighting a war while his male heir was still a child, and then his widow would rule as queen regent on her son's behalf. There was a time, in the 980s, when queen regents were ruling nearly all of Europe.

Marriage for noble and royal women was traditionally a way of establishing kinship and political alliances. Queens were expected to be able to influence their husbands. In the early part of the Middle Ages, before the conversion of most of Europe to Christianity, pagan kings often married Christian princesses. Afterward, the pagan kings usually converted to Christianity. Thus, the Christian queen Clothild converted her pagan husband Clovis, king of the Franks, in 496. Pope Gregory wrote a letter to Queen Bertha, who was married to the Saxon King Ethelbert of Kent, in 597. Pope Boniface wrote a letter to Bertha's daughter Queen Ethelberga, who was married to King Edwin of Northumbria, in 625. Each urged the queens to persuade their husbands to accept Christianity. Both kings were converted.

"EXCEPTIONAL WOMEN"

It was believed that a man could greatly improve his lot in life by marrying a woman of good sense and good character. Conversely, he could make things difficult for himself by marrying a woman who was lazy, disloyal, or indiscreet. The "exceptional woman" was a popular character type in Norse sagas, and she often had great influence over her husband. One character, based on a real historical woman, was Queen Sigrid of Sweden, who persuaded her husband to carry out an act of revenge. King Olaf's saga recounts with grim humor that in about 993, Sigrid was sought in marriage by King Harald of Grenland and King Vissavald of Kiev at the same time. She arranged for both kings and their men to be accommodated in a large hall. She then had her forces attack the hall in the middle of the night and set it on fire. Everyone who escaped from the fire was cut down by her men. Both kings were killed. Sigrid said, "That

Shown here is an image of the marriage of King Philip III of France to Mary of Brabant, now part of modern Belgium. Noblewomen assured their social position through marital arrangements.

ELEANOR OF AQUITAINE

A review of the great queens of medieval Europe would not be complete without mentioning the extraordinary Eleanor of Aquitaine. Eleanor's life story is amazing. She was born in 1122, the daughter of Duke William X of Aquitaine. After the death of her brother in 1130, she became one of the greatest heirs in history. She was married at the age of fifteen to the young king Louis VII of France. Louis was a gentle, melancholy person who had expected to enter the church. The death of his older brother, Philippe, unexpectedly made him heir to the throne, but he continued to be exceptionally pious and devout. He was different from the cultured, sophisticated, and fun-loving men Eleanor was used to. The marriage was not a success. Eleanor is reported to have said, "I have married a monk, not a king." She went on a Crusade to the Holy Land with Louis from 1146 to 1149 and was said to have had a passionate affair with her own uncle, Prince Raymond of Antioch. Louis certainly thought so. He abducted her from Raymond's palace and left suddenly for Jerusalem. After fifteen years together, the couple had produced two daughters but no sons.

In 1152, Eleanor persuaded Louis to have their marriage annulled. He would then be free to find a younger wife who

Eleanor of Aquitaine (1122–1204) was the wife of Louis VII of France and later married Henry II of England in 1152. Besides her marriages, she was considered one of the most powerful rulers of the medieval era in her own right.

(*CONTINUED ON THE NEXT PAGE*)

(CONTINUED FROM THE PREVIOUS PAGE)

could bear him sons. By the terms of the settlement, the two little princesses remained with their father, but Eleanor retained her vast fiefdom in the south of France and could remarry, with Louis's consent. Less than eight weeks after the annulment—and without Louis's consent—to the scandal of everyone, Eleanor married Henry Plantagenet, the young duke of Normandy. She was thirty years old, and he was eighteen. He was also, through his mother, Matilda, the heir to the throne of England. Eleanor and Henry were jointly crowned king and queen in December 1154. Their marriage united the kingdom of England with her enormous territories in the south of France and her husband's in the north, creating an empire much greater than that ruled by the king of France, an imbalance that led to three hundred years of warfare. Even more galling to her ex-husband, she bore the virile Henry eight children during the next twelve years, five of whom were boys.

Eleanor participated actively in the business of government, often acting as Henry's deputy in England while he spent months touring his domains in France. She also made similar tours in her own territories, receiving homage from her vassals, hearing pleas, holding court, granting lands, enacting legislation, and appointing officers. She was passionately fond of hunting. She loved music. Her courts were always full of foreign visitors, musicians, poets, and minstrels. She loved the newest things in literature, culture, and fashion.

Her relationship with Henry later deteriorated. She was very close to her sons, and when she took their part in a rebellion against Henry, he found it necessary to keep her prisoner for sixteen years. After his death, Eleanor returned to power during the reign of her son, King Richard I of England. She acted as regent for some of the time that he was away on a Crusade. She was largely responsible for collecting the huge ransom demanded when he was captured by Leopold of Austria on his way home. Richard died in her arms in 1199, and she continued to support her younger son, King John, before dying peacefully at her favorite abbey of Fontevrault in 1204, at the age of eighty-two. During her long life, she survived illness and intrigue, ambush and abduction, to become a key political figure in twelfth-century Europe.

will teach petty kings from other countries to come wooing me." After that, she was known as Sigrid the Strong-Minded.

THE ERA OF COURTLY ROMANCE

One of the most fashionable and influential of the new forms of literature in the twelfth century was the outpouring of poems, songs, and stories about courtly love. The concept of courtly love permanently influ-

This illustration from the *Codex Manesse* poetry collection shows the thirteenth-century German poet Reinman Der Alte reading a poem to his beloved.

enced our culture and society—and the way we think about romantic love.

In the south of France from around 1100 on, poets began to write in a new way about romantic love between men and women. Before this, poetry was mostly about war, blood feuds, treachery, and loyalty. It was a man's world, and poetry paid little attention to women or love. But the new poets, who were called "troubadours" or "finders," wrote about romantic love as if it were the most important thing in life. If a man loved a woman, he became obsessed with her. If she did not love him back or if, as was often the case, she was too far above him socially, he would become ill with longing. If she offered him encouragement, he would become overjoyed and would submit himself totally to her will. This sort of love had little to do with getting married. It was really an elaborate game played in secret by sophisticated, wealthy aristocratic people with a lot of leisure time.

By 1180, everyone was so familiar with the characteristics of the new style of love that a man called

Andreas Capellanus (André the Chaplain) wrote a long Latin treatise on it called *De arte honesti amandi* ("On the art of honorable loving"). It gives examples of what true love is, and through dialogues and stories, it demonstrates how a man can seduce women of various social backgrounds. Capellanus says that love affairs should ideally take place outside marriage, be conducted in total secrecy, and be accompanied by passionate jealousy. He shows us a courtly society in which people enjoyed debating the rights and wrongs of romantic love in mock court cases, to be finally judged by great ladies. Two of these great ladies were Eleanor of Aquitaine and her daughter Marie, countess of Champagne. He has Marie deliver a famous judgment on one case, stating that it is impossible for true love to exist between people who are married to one another.

LONG-DISTANCE MARRIAGE

There are countless poems and letters by great ladies from the twelfth century onward describing the joys and agonies of love and referring to love affairs they are having with people who are clearly not their husbands. Some historians doubt that these love affairs actually happened because it would have been dangerous for women to engage in them. Their husbands could divorce them on the grounds of adultery, and their lovers could be executed for treason. It was extremely important for a lord to have sons—and to

This image from the *Justiniani in Fortiatum*, a fourteenth-century Latin law manuscript, shows a ruler presiding over the court appearance of a woman accused of adultery.

be certain that they were his own. However, great ladies like Eleanor spent little time with their husbands and certainly had the opportunity for love affairs. In the early part of her marriage to King Henry, Eleanor would see him about twice a year, usually at Christmas and Easter. Most years, she had a baby nine months after these meetings, so she spent much of her time pregnant. During her pregnancy, it would of course be perfectly safe for her to have affairs with other men. Henry was notorious for his own womanizing and fathered many illegitimate children.

It was in the nature of marriages among the aristocracy and gentry for the husband and wife to spend time apart. Husbands had to go to war, attend the royal court, conduct legal business, and supervise their estates in other parts of the country. While they were away, their wives were in charge, sometimes even defending their castles and manor houses against attack.

A family of landowners in fifteenth-century England named Paston preserved hundreds of letters between various family members that present a detailed picture of the trust and partnership between husbands and wives in this kind of marriage. Margaret Mautby married John Paston in 1440. She kept in constant touch with her husband, reporting what she had been doing on his behalf. Her letters are full of busy activity. She supervised servants and farm laborers. She collected rents and debts, oversaw harvests, sold crops and livestock, negotiated with farmers, and took legal action against John Paston's many enemies. She held meetings with tenants, instructed agents to buy and sell, attended court, petitioned justices, and conducted long and complicated marriage negotiations for her children. She often asked her husband in London to buy things for her, mostly cloth, hats, gloves, belts, shoes, stockings, and all kinds of spices and imported food—treacle, pepper, ginger, cloves, cinnamon, mace, oranges, and dates. She even told her husband how much he ought to pay for these goods—and not to buy them if they were too expensive!

CHAPTER THREE

WOMEN, EDUCATION, AND THE CHURCH

One big pillar of religious life in the Middle Ages, part of both the Catholic and Orthodox Christian traditions, was monasticism. This was the tradition of men and women separating from society at large and living lives together in service to God. Men who did this became monks, and entered monasteries. These were large buildings, or a collection of buildings where members of these communities lived and worked. Women who joined such enclosed communities were called nuns. They entered convents, nunneries, or abbeys. Many such communities—also known as orders—still exist today.

Saint Benedict (c. 480–c. 550) had devised the first code of conduct for people wishing to be monks and nuns. Known as the Benedictine Rule, it was based on three principles that all monks and nuns made a solemn vow to keep: poverty, chastity, and obedience. Monks and nuns were not allowed to own personal property. They shared all their goods in common. They were not allowed to marry or have

This fresco shows the order of Poor Clares (the Order of Saint Claire) in a choir. The Poor Clares were founded by Clare of Assisi in Assisi, Italy, in 1212. Religious orders were one of the options open to women to thrive beyond the parameters of marriage.

sexual relationships. And they had to obey their abbot or abbess and follow the Benedictine Rule strictly. The submission of the individual's will and pride was essential for his or her salvation.

The rule divided the day up into periods of work, study, and prayer. The daily round contained seven "offices," or church services, which all members of the community were expected to attend. The first one was at 2 AM and was called *matins*, based on the Latin word for "morning." In most abbeys, the nuns slept together in one large room called a dormitory.

It had stairs leading down directly into the abbey church. The nuns would troop down the stairs and sit in the choir of their church to sing and pray for three hours. Matins was followed directly by *lauds*, based on the word for "praise." Then the nuns could go back to bed and sleep for about three hours, before getting up again for the next service, *prime*, at about 9 AM. After prime, the nuns would go to their chapter house for a general assembly meeting. There they would discuss any business matters and their tasks for the day, and there also the abbess would discipline anyone who had broken the Benedictine Rule. The other services—*tierce*, *sext*, *none*, *vespers*, and *compline*—followed at roughly three-hour intervals. After tierce, at about noon, the nuns went to their dining room, called the refectory, to eat a midday meal. Their food was supposed to be simple—cheese, fish, bread, beans, and a measure of wine or ale. Nuns were not allowed to eat meat unless they were ill. While they ate, one of them would read aloud from the Benedictine Rule, a story of a saint's life, or some other religious text.

A LIFE OF LABOR

Between the offices, the nuns were to supposed to work. The abbess was in charge of everything. The prioress was her second in command. Other nuns were responsible for doing various jobs and reporting to the abbess. The sacristan was in charge of the church and its contents—altar cloths, priests' vestments, candles, incense, the church's chalice, and other precious objects. The cellaress was in charge of the food, drink, and servants; the maintenance of the buildings; and the running of the abbey's lands, farms, produce, and staff. The infirmaress was in charge of the infirmary, where elderly or sick nuns and servants stayed. She prepared all the medicines and ointments to treat them. Some nuns specialized in fine needlework. Some were teachers and took in

This weathered detail of a fresco (created around the eleventh century) is from the tower of the Torba Monastery, or Torba Abbey, in Gornate Olona, Italy, and shows a group of Benedictine nuns.

children to educate. Some copied out, decorated, and illustrated beautiful and valuable manuscripts of the Bible and prayer books called Books of Hours. Some cared for sick people and made herbal remedies. Some nuns studied and wrote books themselves. All abbeys had servants to do the most menial tasks because the nuns tended to be noble women who were not inclined to clean, cook, or tend animals.

The number of women who were able to become nuns was always small, less than half of 1 percent of the female population. Part of the reason for this was that a woman needed to be wealthy to become a nun. When a woman became a nun, she was said to be a bride of Christ, and like other brides she had to bring a dowry with her. A substantial gift of money, goods, or lands to the abbey or convent was required from every member of its community. So, nuns usually came from noble and wealthy families. A woman could become a nun at any time in her life, so long as she was not still married. Many nuns and abbesses entered convents after their husbands had died and their children had grown up, as a kind of second career. Some women, during the early part of the Middle Ages, were put into convents by their families as little children.

The family of Hildegard of Bingen, for example, dedicated their tenth child, little Hildegard, to a religious life when she was seven years old. But in the twelfth century, the practice of offering "child oblates," as these children were called, was stopped. More often, a woman would enter a convent in her teens or early twenties, and she would spend at least a year there before committing herself fully by taking her monastic vows. During this trial period, she was called a novice or postulant and did not wear the nun's habit.

A PATH TO STATUS AND EDUCATION

Since women could not be priests or hold any other kind of public office, becoming an abbess was one way in which a competent, energetic woman could hold an important position, wield authority, and occasionally influence public affairs. Abbesses, particularly if they were members of royal families, could be powerful and influential women and make their mark on history. The famous abbess Hilda of Whitby, who died in 680, was one such woman. Hilda ruled over a double monastery for monks and nuns. It became famous, and she trained five future bishops, all of them outstanding for their capabilities and their holiness. In her time, she was probably the most influential woman in England.

For less famous individuals, the great attraction of life in a convent, at least in the early Middle Ages, was that it gave access to education. Once the nuns had learned to read and write in Latin, the world of learning opened up to them. Many abbeys had libraries of books, which they lent to one another and made copies of. Some abbeys specialized in copying manuscripts and had a *scriptorium*, a workshop

An alterpiece from 1898 depicts the arrival of Hildegard of Bingen at the abbey of Disibodenberg with her family. For her contributions to natural history, Pope Bendedict XVI canonized her on October 7, 2012.

where nuns prepared parchment, ruled lines, mixed inks and paints, ground gold leaf, and set to work. The illuminated manuscripts created there are treasured works of art.

Nunneries were not able to maintain these high standards of learning in the late Middle Ages. Fewer people were making large gifts of land and money. Nuns found it harder to attract good teachers, and many were no longer fluent in Latin. Some convents were reported to be lax about following the Benedictine Rule. Nuns, it was said, were dressing in fine, fashionable clothing, eating expensive delicacies, keeping pet dogs and monkeys, gossiping and chattering through the divine service, and flirting with men. There were reforming movements that began in the thirteenth century. Saint Francis of Assisi's friend and disciple, Saint Clare, founded a new order for women. Saint Francis wanted to return to the early ideal of poverty. He could see that many older established monasteries had grown lax and corrupt.

The Cloister of the Convent of St. Domenic in Perugia, Italy, shows the typical architecture of many monastic buildings of the medieval period. It now serves as the National Archaeological Museum.

They were like clubs for wealthy people. He wanted monks and nuns to preach to and care for the poor, as Christ had done, and he insisted that poverty should be real and not theoretical. Saint Clare,

EXTREME DEVOTION: BECOMING AN ANCHORESS

There were other ways for women to follow a religious life besides joining a convent. It was common in the Celtic church during the early Middle Ages for women to withdraw from everyday life and live apart from people in simple huts or even caves, as female hermits. The women would spend their days praying and meditating, and local people would provide them with food and clothes because of their holiness. Many of these early Celtic recluses were considered to be saints while they were still alive. This custom was eventually institutionalized by the church. A woman could decide to become an anchoress. She would be enclosed in a cell, usually built into the side of a church or monastery, with a little window into the church so that she could receive Holy Communion. As she was dead to the world, a priest read the burial service over her as the door was bricked up. She never left the cell. Her food and drink and supplies were given to her through a small opening in the wall.

Julian of Norwich (1342–1416), whose image adorns this part of the Church of Saints Mary and Andrew in Langham, England, was an English anchoress and theologian of the fourteenth century.

too, shared this ideal and wrote her own rule for her nuns. Anyone wishing to join had to first give away all her possessions to the poor, including her clothes, and cut off all her hair. The rule was accepted by the church in Rome in 1253, just two days before Clare herself died.

From the twelfth century onward, women who could not afford to join a convent or who did not wish to shut themselves away from the world in a cell invented a new kind of religious life. They practiced the life of a working woman as they worshiped God. They volunteered to live simply and to prepare themselves for heaven by doing good works. Sometimes they joined together and lived in a group with other women, sometimes not. They called themselves Beguines. This movement arose spontaneously in the area that is now Belgium and the Netherlands and became widespread throughout northern Europe in the late Middle Ages. The women mostly worked in the

cloth industry—the main industry of that region—as fullers or weavers, and any surplus money they earned they gave to the poor. They got up early in the morning to hear mass, and after work in the evening, they went back to church or met in one another's rooms for prayers and meditations. They wore plain clothes, usually gray, and ate simple food. The church did not know what to make of this movement at first because it had arisen from the desires of the women themselves and not from the leadership of the church, but eventually it gave its approval. Throughout the Middle Ages, women were being celebrated for their religious lives and holiness, and nearly all the church's female saints date from the medieval period.

CHAPTER FOUR

WOMEN AT WORK

Anglo-Saxon surnames common in the United States, the United Kingdom, and other English-speaking nations reveal the working roots of many people's ancestors. People with the family names Webster and Weaver were tied to the craft of weaving. The names Brewer and Brewster arose from the practice of brewing ale. The once popular term for an older, unmarried woman, "spinster," came from the fact that many women worked spinning wool or flax into thread for textiles. Studies of these names—along with evidence from medieval wills, contracts, lawsuits, marriage settlements, and medical and financial records—paint a picture of women in the Middle Ages being hardworking and, at times, even equal partners with men. Some participated in the trades and professions and became entrepreneurs.

WOMEN AND GUILDS

Women provided the core of the workforce in the production of cloth, particularly in spinning and weaving. It was a complicated process, involving different stages of specialized work. For all these specialized trades there was a guild, an association of craftsmen or craftswomen who agreed on certain rules. The rules enforced fair dealings between tradesperson and customer, and tradesperson and apprentice, and ensured proper quality standards. Most guild members and officials were men. Some cities and towns excluded women from guild membership, but some allowed women to become guild members, especially if they were widows carrying on their dead husbands' businesses. Some allowed women to set up a business on their own, even if they were still married.

Some silk-making guilds had only women members. For example, in Paris in about 1270, a man named Etienne de Boileau wrote down all the regulations of the craft guilds of Paris, including those of the all-female silk-makers guild. From this we see that a woman wanting to be a silk-maker needed to apprentice herself to a mistress in the craft for a minimum of six years. While an apprentice, she promised to be faithful to her mistress, honest, and well behaved, and not give away secrets of the trade. After that, she had learned enough to be employed as a journeywoman who could hire herself out. She had to work for at least a year and a day at this level, to perfect herself in her craft and learn

Women are shown weaving in this illustration from a fourteenth-century edition of *Ovide Moralise*, a collection of works from the ancient Roman poet Ovid, who became popular in the medieval era.

the regulations. Then she could call herself a mistress of the craft and set up her own workshop, employ her own journeywomen, and take on her own apprentices, but not more than two at a time. Silk-makers were not allowed to work at night or on public holidays. They were not allowed to mix wool threads or foil in with the silk, or the work would be declared "false and bad" and would be burned. There were overseers to enforce these regulations. Infringements were punished by fines.

Women were also prominent in the wool industry, which was central to commercial life in northern Europe,

This architectural relief on the Florence Cathedral, *The Art of Weaving*, shows the importance of the craft among medieval women.

as well as to other industries. There are records of women in towns and cities throughout medieval Europe working as fullers, dyers, tanners, glovers, shoemakers, purse-makers, cap-makers, embroiderers, and lace-makers, as well as merchants and traders.

In Southampton, England, women were even employed packing wool in bales and loading it onto ships in the docks. As well as bakers and brewers, women often worked as butchers and fishmongers. They often sold food and drink at markets and fairs or in their own shops and alehouses. Special courts had the job of making certain that every tradesman and tradeswoman who provided food or drink for sale was selling good, fresh food in the right amounts and with the right ingredients. Anyone who was caught trying to defraud people was arrested and fined. In 1364, for example, Alice de Caudstone was accused of using a false measure to serve ale to her customers. The court found that she had built up the bottom of her quart jug with an inch and a half of pitch so that the jug contained much less than a quart. She had to stand in the women's pillory, called the thewe. The cheating woman food seller, and especially the cheating alewife, was a stereotype in medieval stories and pictures.

IN MEDICINE

There was another profession in which women were known to work, and that was medicine. Poor people might have the advice and experience of an older woman in their community who had nursed people through illnesses and who had some knowledge of herbal remedies. Women had traditionally nursed the sick and attended women in childbirth. It was natural for this body of knowledge to accumulate and be passed on through them. This sort of woman in later centuries, however, might be burned as a witch. Women were excluded from studying at universities. And they found it harder to qualify and to be licensed as actual doctors, but they still practiced, right up to the end of the period.

The most renowned school of medicine in Europe was at Salerno in Italy. In its earliest days, this school had as one of its professors a famous woman doctor called Trotula. She wrote an influential book called De passionibus mulieres (On the diseases of women), probably some time in the mid-twelfth century. The book mainly deals with problems of fertility, pregnancy, and labor and birth, although it also covers other diseases suffered by

THE CASE OF JACOBA FELICIA

A woman doctor named Jacoba Felicia was sued by the dean and faculty of medicine at the University of Paris in 1322 for persistently examining and treating sick people, despite several previous warnings, when she had no license to practice. Felicia brought many witnesses to testify that she had successfully cured their illnesses. Felicia argued forcefully that the law requiring doctors to be licensed was more than one hundred years old and that it had been enacted to protect people from ignorant quacks and charlatans who had no idea what they were doing. She herself was obviously a different matter, being highly skilled and experienced. She added that it was useful to have a woman doctor to treat women and their diseases because many women were too modest to allow male doctors to examine them and many had died from their illnesses rather than permit this. The court was obviously impressed by her eloquent arguments, but it still upheld the university's case. Felicia was unlicensed and would have to leave Paris.

women. It shows considerable knowledge of the subject and gives midwives practical advice on how to induce labor, how to turn the fetus in the womb, what to do if the baby has died before birth, and so on. It advises pregnant women to eat a healthy diet and to exercise. It anticipates many therapies that are used today to help women give birth. Trotula also has advice on how to get rid of lice, worms, bad breath, toothache, rough skin, freckles, and wrinkles!

From the twelfth and thirteenth centuries onward, male doctors increasingly took over the practice of medicine. A doctor had to be licensed by a medical school or university to practice, which had the effect of excluding women from the profession. However, records show that some women doctors continued to practice. In 1408, a woman doctor named Joanna treated two monks at Westminster Abbey in London and was paid three shillings and a sixpence for the medicines she gave them. A woman doctor named Joan du Lee petitioned King Henry IV of England in the early 1400s for a license to practice medicine "all about the country without hindrance by all folk."

LITERARY WOMEN

Some of the best-known writers and poets from the Middle Ages were women. Among the troubadour poets of southern France who composed passionate love poetry were twelve female poets, known as *trobairitz*. A twelfth-century woman known to us only as Marie de France wrote some of the most exquisite short romances, called Breton lais. Many

This illumination from *Scivias*, illustrated by Hildegard of Bingen in 1151, depicts her receiving a holy vision.

more women writers were nuns, like the astonishingly talented abbess Hildegard of Bingen, who wrote theological treatises, medical handbooks, poems and songs, and beautiful choral music, as well as numerous letters and an account of her long and eventful life. Christine de Pizan was the first woman we know to have made her living entirely as a professional writer, after being widowed at the age of twenty-five with three young children and numerous other relatives to support. Christine wrote many books about her own life and activities and also took a conscious stand against the many male writers of the Middle Ages who attacked women as inferior and sinful creatures. Christine dared to state that women had the same moral worth and were capable of as much heroic conduct as men. She proved it with her collection of tales of great women, *The Book of the City of Ladies*, and her later

Writer, poet, and biographer Christine de Pizan is shown here lecturing to a group of men. She was arguably Europe's first professional woman writer.

manual of instruction for women of all classes, *The Treasure of the City of Ladies*. She also wrote poems, a biography of King Charles V, a history of the world, a book on chivalry and warfare, another on government, and several moral treatises.

Women also worked as painters and illustrators. Christine mentions in one of her books that the most expert artist of miniature paintings then working in Paris was a woman named Anastasia. Christine knew her well and had commissioned her to paint detailed flower borders and decorations for her own manuscripts. There are records of numerous other women miniature painters and scribes.

GLOSSARY

anchoress A woman who lived a life of prayer apart from the world in a secluded place.
apprentice Someone who learns a trade by working under a more experienced mentor.
aristocrat A person of the highest social rank.
ballad A song or poem that tells a story.
cesspit A large covered hole in the ground where garbage and sewage gathers before it is disposed of periodically.
chastity Abstaining from sexual relations.
chattel A person's movable possessions, as opposed to a house or property.
convent A Christian monastic community where nuns live and work.
Crusades A series of military campaigns waged by European Christians during the Middle Ages.
dowry Money or property brought by a bride to her husband or his family when they marry.
estate A large area of land owned by one person.
fuller A person who cleans and thickens cloth.
gentry People who owned land but did not have noble titles.
heretic A person who challenges or opposes the beliefs of the church.
medieval Relating to the Middle Ages, from about 500 CE to about 1500 CE.
nobility A group of people of high social rank.
pagan Refers to European peoples who believe in pre-Christian deities.

peasant A poor farmer with low social status.
prophetic Saying what will happen in the future.
regent A person who rules a country on behalf of the actual ruler when the ruler is still too young to rule or has fallen ill.
sect A smaller group within a larger religion or faith that has different beliefs or practices.
tanner A person who tans animal skins into leather.
textile Cloth or woven fabric.
troubadour A medieval lyric poet who composed and sang as his vocation, with the tradition originating in southern France and employing Old Occitan, or Provençal, as the language of composition.
vassal A person who provided military or political support to a higher-ranking lord in exchange for land.

Canadian Society of Medievalists
c/o Roisin Cossar
Department of History
University of Manitoba
454 Fletcher Argue Building
Winnipeg, MB R3T 5V5
Canada
Website: http://www.canadianmedievalists.ca
The Canadian Society of Medievalists is an academic organization dedicated to promoting excellence in research for all aspects of medieval studies.

Columbia University Medieval Colloquium
602 Philosophy Hall
Columbia University
New York, NY 10027
Website: http://blogs.cuit.columbia.edu/medguild
The Medieval Colloquium (formerly the Medieval Guild) of Columbia University is a graduate student organization for medievalists whose mission is to help students develop professionally in their research about this historical period.

Medieval Academy of America
17 Dunster Street, Suite 202
Cambridge, MA 02138
(617) 491-1622
Website: http://www.medievalacademy.org
The Medieval Academy of America is the largest organi-

zation in the United States promoting excellence in medieval studies, including fostering research, publication, and teaching in medieval art archaeology, history, law, literature, music, philosophy, religion, science, social and economic institutions.

Medieval Association of the Pacific
c/o Michael Hanly, President
Department of English
Washington State University
Avery Hall 471
Pullman, WA 99164
(509) 335-4081
Website: http://www.medievalpacific.org
The Medieval Association of the Pacific is an organization of university faculty, students, and independent scholars from around the Pacific Rim, including North America, Japan, Australia, and New Zealand, founded to support interdisciplinary medieval studies.

National Women's History Museum
Administrative Offices
205 S. Whiting Street, Suite 254
Alexandria, VA 22304
(703) 461-1920
https://www.nwhm.org
The National Women's History Museum researches, collects and exhibits the contributions of women to the social, cultural, economic and political life of the United States in the context of world history.

Society for Medieval Feminist Scholarship (SMFS)
Professor Liz Herbert McAvoy, President
College of Arts and Humanities
219 Keir Hardie
Swansea University
Singleton Park
Swansea SA2 8PP
Wales
Website: http://smfsweb.org
The Society for Medieval Feminist Scholarship (SMFS) promotes the study of early Christianity, the Middle Ages, and the Early Modern era from the perspective of gender studies, women's studies, and feminist studies, and actively promotes and supports interdisciplinary exchanges at all levels of higher education.

WEBSITES

Because of the changing number of Internet links, Rosen Publishing has developed an online list of websites related to the subject of this book. This site is updated regularly. Please use this link to access this list:

http://www.rosenlinks.com/LMID/women

FOR FURTHER READING

Baer, Ann. *Medieval Woman: Village Life in the Middle Ages* (Everyday Life of Women through History). London, UK: Michael O'Mara Books, 2012.

Gies, Joseph, and Frances Gies. *Women in the Middle Ages: The Lives of Real Women in a Vibrant Age of Transition*. New York, NY: HarperCollins, 2010.

Jackson, Deirdre. *Medieval Women*. London, UK: British Library Publishing, 2015.

Leon, Vicki. *Outrageous Women of the Middle Ages*. New York, NY: John Wiley & Sons, 1998.

Leyser, Henrietta. *Medieval Women*. Irvine, CA: Phoenix Press, 2002.

Leyser Henrietta. *Medieval Women: Social History Of Women In England 450-1500* (Women in History). London, UK: Weidenfeld & Nicolson, 2013.

Morrison, Susan Signe. *A Medieval Woman's Companion: Women's Lives in the European Middle Ages*. Oxford, UK: Oxbow Books, 2015.

Mount, Toni. *The Medieval Housewife, and Other* Women of the Middle Ages. Stroud, UK: Amberley Publishing, 2015.

Phillips, Kim M. *A Cultural History of Women in the Middle Ages* (The Cultural Histories Series). New York, NY: Bloomsbury, 2016.

Singman, Jeffrey L. *The Middle Ages: Everyday Life in Medieval Europe*. New York, NY: Sterling, 2013.

Weir, Allison. *Eleanor of Aquitaine: A Life*. New York, NY: Ballantine Books, 2012.

BIBLIOGRAPHY

Amt, Emilie. *Women's Lives in Medieval Europe: A Sourcebook*. New York, NY: Routledge, 1993.

Bardsley, Sarah. *Women's Roles in the Middle Ages* (Women's Roles Through History). Westport, CT: Greenwood Publishing, 2007.

Bruckner, Matilda Tomaryn. *Songs of the Women Troubadours*. Irvine, CA: Garland, 1995.

Comnena, Anna, and E.R.A. Sewter, trans. *The Alexiad*. New York, NY: Penguin Books, 1969.

Cosman, Madeleine Pelner. *Women at Work in Medieval Europe*. New York, NY: Facts on File, 2000.

Erler, Mary C., and Maryanne Kowaleski, eds. *Women and Power in the Middle Ages*. Athens, GA: University of Georgia Press, 2004.

Flanagan, Sabine. *Hildegard of Bingen: A Visionary Life*. New York, NY: Routledge, 1989.

Green, Monica Helen. *The Trotula: An English Translation of the Medieval Compendium of Women's Medicine*. Philadelphia, PA: University of Pennsylvania Press, 2001.

Larrington, Carolyne. *Women and Writing in Medieval Europe: A Sourcebook*. New York, NY: Routledge, 1995.

Power, Eileen. *Medieval Women*. Cambridge, UK: Cambridge University Press, 1995.

Vernade, Bruce L. *Women's Monasticism and Medieval Society*. Ithaca, NY: Cornell University Press, 1999.

INDEX

ABOUT THE AUTHORS

Margaux Baum is a writer and editor from Queens, New York.

Andrea Hopkins won an open scholarship to study at Oxford University and gained a double first in English there. She wrote a doctoral thesis on penitence in medieval romance, which later formed the basis for her monograph *The Sinful Knights*, published in 1990 by Oxford University Press, where she now works. She is also the author of *Knights*, *The Chronicles of King Arthur*, *The Book of Courtly Love*, *Heroines*, *The Book of Guinevere*, *Harald the Ruthless: Last of the Vikings*, and *Most Wise and Valiant Ladies*. She is mad about medieval art, literature, and history. She lives in Oxford.

PHOTO CREDITS

Cover (silhouetted figures), p. 23 © Ivy Close Images/Alamy Stock Photo; cover (background) Tomasz Bidermann/Shutterstock.com; p. 3 Heather McCallum/Moment/Getty Images; pp. 4–5 (background) leoks/Shutterstock.com; p. 5 Universal Images Group/Hulton Fine Art/Getty Images; pp. 7, 21, 35, 46 Bildagentur Zoonar GmbH/Shutterstock.com; p. 10 Archivo Catedral de Tarazona, Zaragoza, Aragon, Spain/Index/Bridgeman Images; p. 11 British Library, London, UK/© British Library Board. All Rights Reserved/Bridgeman Images; p. 13 DEA Picture Library/Getty Images; p. 18 DEA/G. Dagli Orti/De Agostini Picture Library/Getty Images; p. 25 British Library, London, UK/Bridgeman Images; p. 27 Archive Photos/Getty Images; p. 30 Photo © Tarker/Bridgeman Images; p. 32 Biblioteca Monasterio del Escorial, Madrid, Spain/Bridgeman Images; p. 36 Universal History Archive/Universal Images Group/Getty Images; p. 38 DEA/A. Dagli Orti/De Agostini Picture Library/Getty Images; p. 41 Historisches Museum, Bingen, Germany/Bildarchiv Steffens/Bridgeman Images; p. 42 DEA/C. Sappa/De Agostini Picture Library/Getty Images; p. 44 Photo © Neil Holmes/ Bridgeman Images; p. 48 Bibliotheque Municipale, Rouen, France/Bridgeman Images; p. 49 © The Print Collector/Alamy Stock Photos; p. 53 Private Collection/Getty Images; p. 54 New York Public Library/Science Source/Getty Images; cover and interior pages flourishes and borders wenani/Shutterstock.com; interior pages fleur-de-lis riedjal/Shutterstock.com; interior pages textures murengstockphoto/Shutterstock.com, LeksusTuss/Shutterstock.com; back cover (background) © iStockphoto.com/MagMos; back cover (silhouette) Dikas Studio/Shutterstock.com.

Designer: Michael Moy; Editor: Philip Wolny; Photo Researcher: Philip Wolny